THE ROAD TO CONSCIOUSNESS

words of inspiration from a spirit guide

by Jeanne Livingston

Jeanne Livingston
PO Box 422
Garrison, NY 10524

Cover and book design by Jerry Gross
Back cover photography by John D. Svirsky
Drawings by Jeanne Livingston
Edited by Brian Arcarese

The Road to Consciousness.
Copyright © 2013 by Jeanne Livingston.
All rights reserved.
ISBN 978-0-615-86619-2

Printed in the United States of America

Published by: Manitou Publishing
PO Pox 422; Garrison, NY 10524

Special acknowledgment and thanks
to John D. Svirsky, whose love,
support, encouragement, and work
helped materialize this book.
And to my close friends, you know
who you are, who help me along
my road to consciousness.

TABLE OF CONTENTS

INTRODUCTION

Often the truth is so strange that it's difficult to communicate believably to others. In my case much of the help I received toward consciousness came from discarnate beings, otherwise known as spirit guides. I received the love, patience, encouragement and acceptance from the spirit world that most people get from their families, religion, schools or everyday lives in general. Perhaps this happened because I was an " army brat ", changing schools and locations every year from ages four to eleven. Or maybe my Capricorn stubbornness accounts for being prisoner to my five senses for so long, or just maximum family pressures cracked me open...but one day, instead of heading toward the depressing outer rims of darkness, I turned inward and began my journey toward the Light.

Spirit guides and I have interacted through telepathy and mediums over many years. Most of the material in this book was channeled through Alexander Murray, a fabulous New York City medium who refers to himself as " medium rare", and I attended trance-sitting classes weekly which at that time were given in his home.

A medium, for those unfamiliar with the term, is a person who permits other entities to use his or her body...entities who presently have no physical vehicle and therefore no direct way to communicate with humans. The medium agrees to leave his or her body through entering into a trance state and thereby allows spirits to use his/her faculties. Some mediums channel only one entity, others many. For the medium, entering a trance state is like letting a friend use your home while you're away; your home, in this case, being your physical body.

I first met Prahsingh at Alex's classes and it took time for our relationship to grow. As with any two individuals making friends, we had to sense each other and build trust. I remember on his second visit to class asking him to spell his name and tell me about his most recent incarnation on the Earth plane. He answered that his name, Prahsingh, means "Brother Lion" in English, and that he had been a Buddhist priest at the Chaing Mai Temple in Thailand during the 16th century. In time we grew closer as his insight and kindness addressed my deepest fears and disappointments. I learned how to truly listen and my ability to assimilate his wisdom progressed.

Prahsingh is my dear teacher and friend. He has guided me in ways of learning how to put principles above personalities. For, as Prahsingh says: " It is important to know in some way that the great truths are not created by anyone; they're simply understood by some, and communicated through others. We all flatter ourselves to think that we have come upon something unique, but I think it is already there, part of the Universe. It's just that we add our own experience and expression thereby participating in the great infinity we call Creation."

In the far East, the languages have no way of expressing gender. I have tried to preserve Prahsingh's charm by not overediting his words, for he speaks directly to your soul. So often we can't help the terrible things that happen to us; however we can learn how to be responsible and conscious of how we react to them.

During the 26 years that have passed since the 2nd edition of this book, these teachings have automatically filtered into my life. They've helped me be more comfortable within myself and, frankly, nicer. I laugh more, love more and enjoy more as the outside world becomes supermechanized, packaged and driven. The challenges also increase more than ever to stay centered. I thank my lucky stars that so many authors and teachers have shared their wealth of knowledge to help us grow and that now more people can learn through the availability of computers. Therefore, I wish to share precious Prahsingh with you, the reader, in this last edition. The book will help you follow your own spiritual path. And if you call Prahsingh and listen, he will come to you personally, for as the expression goes, "He's the real deal !"

Blessings to you from his Jeanne, the author.

JUDGMENT

I wish to tell you of things I have observed for many, many lifetimes; that is: the need to pass judgment; the need to always have some comment as to the good, the bad, the indifferent...as if to say that it was necessary for everything to be judged, to be labeled and proclaimed. And I tell you this: some things cannot be.

Some things must simply be experienced. They are a mixture of many qualities consisting of good, bad, indifferent and hard to categorize. But if you feel that you must make a value judgment, that it is either a good thing or a bad thing, that it is either worthwhile or not worthwhile, sometimes you will find yourself unable to do this, and find that it is hard to see clearly. Because many good people make bad actions and, from time to time, bad people seem to do good work in spite of themselves. And you can be easily mistaken to think that the bad person who seems to have done a good thing is a good person, and the good person who has made an error is a bad person. And so you see, this is how history has often judged people. Is that not so? Would you not agree with me, or have observed this? The only true judge in the end, perhaps, is history itself, or life; if you like, the gods or however you would express it.

Is anyone ever in a position to judge? No. Only to discern; to know these things as they are taking place and to discern the difference, but not to judge. And those who judge proclaim themselves fools, for they think that they know enough to judge, and no one does. Everyone can discern. They may discern by the powers of reasoning and experience which they have acquired through their many lives. But judge? I think not. Therefore, it is taught by your Christ: "Judge not, lest ye be judged." How wise it is. We have a saying in the East, that no one knows enough to be a judge. It is that simple. But let all discern with their eye and with their heart. Not only with their eye but with their heart. For the eye sees but a part. And your Justice wears a blindfold, so even she does not look at all, but weighs in the balance by the feel of things. And I say that is a better test sometimes than the eye, for the eye is often deceived.

The worst is that which counterfeits good. That is the most difficult. And I'm sorry to say that so many are fooled by this, and so many are fooled by the words that pass for good words because they say good. But, if you listen with your heart, they do not feel good because words have more than sound. Words have meaning, and meaning is not just the sound but how it affects you. You know what I mean .

So if a word coming to you is a pretty word, but it brings

a very unpretty understanding, then there perhaps you must understand that the word alone is nothing. It is also how it is uttered and the context in which it is spoken, who speaks it and for what reason. For words are but the means by which communication is affected...one of the means. And for those who do not feel or listen to the quality of the communication, they may easily be used to deceive.

I say that if a person deep within his or her heart seeks truth, he may be deceived for a little while, but in the end enlightenment comes to him. Those who seek to know will be seeing through deceit and through the counterfeit. They will feel that. And in the end, goodness is inevitably vindicated, and wickedness is inevitably seen for what it is, and likewise foolishness.

You have very little you can do to control the way people see you, because it is their eyes that look, and they bring to their observations their experiences and their own egos and their own wills. And if they desire to judge, then they will judge whether you desire it or not. There is nothing you can do to prevent it. If they will see the truth, they will see the truth no matter what you do. You can make an ass out of yourself. You can be a perfect disaster, and those who know the truth will know exactly what is happening to you and will understand, because they are not fooled by false judgments about you. They are not fooled when you make errors. They know a good person when they see one, even when that good person is in error. They bring to the experience understanding or they do not, and a willingness to understand more. They bring an open eye or a closed one. They bring prejudice or they do not. It is not up to you but for one thing...*Be Yourself.*

Do the best you can, but do it as you feel to do it. Be authentic. Do not try to please one and then to please another and try to be different things to different people. That is a big mistake because that only makes it more difficult, though not impossible, for true seekers to know you for what you are. Even they, when you are playing your many faces, will still see through your disguises. But it is better if you are more yourself. Would you not agree?

Be who you are. Those who are meant to understand you, know you and see you for what you are...will, and they will have a better chance of seeing that quickly and come to your aid and support. Those who are not predisposed to like you never will; no matter how much you seek to please them, you never can. Because they have it in their minds not to be pleased by you, not to like you. And even if you try, they may accept your efforts but hold you in contempt. So do not even make the effort, I tell you.

I hope this suggestion will be useful.

COMPASSION

My friends, there is a problem that many of you spiritually ennobled and enlightened souls have; that is one of coming to grips with the revelation, or realization, that most of the world cannot, will not, and does not wish to understand you. Not now, not ever.

That can be very disconcerting and very disappointing. It can produce anger. It can produce many things. Unfortunately, the lesson for all of you who are wiser and who see how the world is foolish, who are kind and see how the world is mean, who are artistic and see how the world is barbaric and have fine, fine sensitivity, whose eyes and ears, whose whole physical instrument is tuned to beauty in the midst of so much which is ugly, crass, objectionable...will you run for the mountains? Will you live in the cave? Will you stop up your ears and blind your eyes so that you will not be offended?

Some of you have developed, I am sorry to say, what is a good but unhealthy contempt for the world around you. Now when I say this word, it may stab at your heart. Forgive me if I sound accusative. I do not mean to. But I think if I am correct, then you will have the proper reaction in your heart, which will say, "Yes, I have contempt." I will not say who does and who does not, but I think, perhaps, it has touched every heart at some time. For I must tell you right now that it is natural under the circumstances.

It would be unnatural for you, almost, not to have it. I would be very surprised, and you would be close to nirvana if you have no contempt from time to time. Because, you see, the world gives you more than ample opportunity, and it gives you more than just cause. So what is the remedy? If you have cause and opportunity, if you are so sensitive and everything around you is so insensitive, what is the remedy?

Well, I must tell you that the great gurus, the great sages of old, had many times more sensitivity than the most sensitive one here, myself included. Yet they could walk in the midst of dirt, of ugliness, of strife, of all manner of trouble...all the most distressing things you could imagine, and some that you could not even imagine because some are more distressing than you have experienced...and maintain an inner peace, a strength and power. How is this done? Well, I mention one name which might be useful; that is Mother Teresa of Calcutta, only to say that she was an enormously sensitive person, but she did not let her sensitivity stand between her and the performance of what she came to do.

We must trade contempt for compassion, my friends.

You must give up your judgment for compassion. I must tell you that it is not difficult for any one of you to do. It is not difficult.

It is no challenge for you to perceive that the world is ugly, for it most certainly is in many respects...at least the human part. The human condition has much that is degenerate and cruel, vice-ridden, etc. Therefore it does not say much for you to have discerned these things. It does not say much for you to have discerned that the world is full of uneducated, boring and unpleasant people. It says much for you if you can say that the world is full of poor and pitiful people who need your help, and that there is a place for you in loving kindness and gentle action to lift them out of their misery. That speaks volumes for you. For when you can see that you have some part to play in the alleviation of all that stupidity, misery, vice, corruption and ugliness, then you have become useful, and more than that, you have become significant.

For that is, perhaps, the only thing that will make you significant is to have some part to play in the alleviation of human suffering. Certainly, those who have good taste do not need you to help them further it. They can take care of that themselves. Certainly, those who are on their way through spiritual evolution find their way, come what may, in the sense that a student who is already in his studies will be highly self-motivated. But those who have not yet seen that to look beyond the end of their nose and to realize that there are other means to solve problems, these are persons for whom you may have some real answers.

Now the reason I am saying this is because if you keep on with the company of spiritually enlightened people, the day will come when you have only yourself to speak to. It becomes a very exclusive and very small circle. You know what I mean? There's little room on top of the mountain, and no great spiritual master ever has isolated himself or herself. The day will come, my friends, when you have to be content with the fact that you cannot expect to have peers, as such, but you must be content yourself always to have a knowledge and a wisdom which you cannot share, as you understand it, but must be shared at the level of understanding that is beneath you.

Remember this, and this is the problem, that so many of you expect or desire that you will have those persons come into your life who are ready and willing and open to receive everything that you have to give, and it will be effortless. But, my friends, the lesson is that *giving is not effortless. Sharing is not effortless.* It requires a great deal of work, and it is sharing not on your terms, but very often on the terms which are dictated not by them or by you but by the reality of the situation.

Remember, it is so important, that if you are truly serving, one of the words that spiritual people are to bring into their vocabulary more is *efficiency*. One wishes to be efficient in sharing, and the most efficient way is to adjust, and to see where is the real need and to make every effort you need to adjust so that you can efficiently perform the work that you have come to do. It is too easy to stand back and say, "They must come to me. They must find me at my level." Perhaps they will never come to your level. It may just be possible that if Buddha had ever said these things, no one would have ever learned from him because he would never have taught anyone. Who was at his level? Had he expected them to be at his level before teaching, they never would have been able to come. Jesus and the rest taught the great unwashed, illiterate multitudes, and they did these things in language that was far beneath the level of their own comprehension. And they were not concerned with teaching others like themselves, but those who were not like themselves.

Therefore, if you have contempt for that which is vulgar, dirty, miserable, mean and stupid, take another look. It may be the very reason why you have come here. It might just present you with your greatest opportunity.
Bless you.

THE FIRST COMMANDMENT

You have in your Judeo-Christian religion something called the Ten Commandments. These were given to Moses by God. They are the tenets of your belief. These are great gifts to the world. They should be understood more than they are. They should be studied in the light of the current times in which you live and be applied to your lives. I could bring you many Eastern teachings, and hold them up to you, but I give to you what you have already, for in it is much wisdom, and we have no better teaching in the East than this. I will speak of the First Commandment: *Thou shalt have no other gods before me.*

What does this God want from you? You know all Ten Commandments were given to you, as people, to live happy lives...better lives. The purpose of the Ten Commandments was for human beings to live in a happy successful world. Right? What other reason were the Commandments given for? They were given for you, not for God. God did not need commandments. God had the truth. God shared the truth with man through the Commandments.

"Thou shalt have no other gods before me." That is a very broad and very full statement. For whatever is your master is your god. Later Jesus said, "You cannot serve two masters well." You cannot serve both God and mammon. In his exposition and explanation of these great laws, Jesus simply tried to redefine them in terms of a world many hundreds or thousands of years after Moses' time. Again it is important to look at the Commandments as they would be interpreted in your lives today.

Who are your gods? What do you worship? What do you obey? For some, fear is a god. For others it is power or money. There are many gods. Is acceptance by your fellow man a god that you obey? Anything that you admit to have power over you, that is greater over you, becomes a god. Some have made images to adore which have shrunk the power of God to the size of a statue; have shrunk the power of God to man's limited form, and therefore it is a disservice.

Later the Commandment "not to bow down before any graven images" relates back to the First Commandment, because any graven image, anything that would seek to define God, would limit God's expression and God's power; for God, *the* God, all and everything, is ultimate authority and power to which all of you have recourse and access.

This Higher Power can help you overcome any intervening gods, if you put it first in your life. Many, in fact, all of the intervening gods are really demons passing as God. They're not God but demi-gods that terrorize and tyrannize you. They do not liberate you. They enslave you. The great God asks service but never enslaves. The lesser gods enslave. How do they enslave? They enslave by obsessing you, by putting all of your attention on the things they represent, whereas the great God is god of all things and incorporates all things into a balanced world. The lesser gods are gods of this or gods of that and obsess you with this or that and rob you of the other things and the proportion of life. The gods of war obsess you with war and battle. The gods of money obsess you with wealth. The gods of power obsess you with power and control. Perhaps, like the seven deadly sins, the demon gods may assume the forms of drink or food or some other substance. They may assume some material form like gold, the god King Midas worshipped.

These are the false idols, the demons which rob you of the inheritance of your own Higher Power. That great spiritual entity is there for you, and if other gods have come up, if false gods and demons have stood between you and that God, step over them. Reach up and out and say: "I will have no other gods before You. I will love You first. I do not know how to forget these others, but I will not forget You, either. I will remember You first." And when these false gods beckon, remember the true God. Always keep that God number one, and you will be out of trouble very quickly. Because when you keep that great God number one, the false gods cannot intervene.

I cannot tell you how great a power this God has. But if you do not acknowledge it, it cannot be there actively for you in your life. I also would say that in loving this God first and remembering this God first, you will quickly forget the false gods. They will fall away, and you will be liberated from their power, and you will have your spiritual center. And let nothing stand between you and that God...not priest, nor church, nor process. But always go directly to It, and you shall find great strength by It.

Meditate on this commandment and know that God, your God and mine, gave this for your good, to be remembered for all time like a beacon light in the midst of darkness. Love that God first, above all things, and the rest shall be added unto you. That is my opinion.

In studying all of the Commandments, let me add; do not be quick to assume things because of them. Language is very strange. What the words meant in olden times must sometimes be considered anew. I think that it is important to read all old teachings with a full knowledge of what the words meant in the time in which they were written. Because you are reading them thousands of years later, you must try to understand what the language of that era conveyed. Language has changed significantly and that must be taken into account.

WORDS

I realize that sometimes I do not speak things as clearly as I might write them, if I had the time to consider my words more carefully before speaking. Ah, that is why speech makes fools of so many.

Were thought to come before the lips were to move, so much grief would be prevented. But too often the words are out before the brain has been put to work. Before the mind considers a thing, one has already spoken of it. Ah, me! I wish to speak to this subject a little if I may.

Your Master Jesus said, "By your tongues you betray yourselves." I think it is an old Indian proverb as well. I do not know who said it first, or when, but it certainly sounds as if the Buddha himself might have said it. To speak without thinking is a very, very dangerous action. It can lead to more trouble than anything else, for few things are so irrevocable as words spoken. Actions, it seems, may be undone, but words are hard to erase. Perhaps you are all being made very much aware of this by certain controversies arising around your political elections and those candidates who are suffering from this particular problem of speaking without thinking first.

Possibly you have all been trained wrongly that you need to answer every inquiry, and that you need for some reason always to give a quick response, that you are thought to be very slow or dim if you do not speak your mind quickly, that you do not provide an instant answer for every question, that you do not hold a lucid opinion at the tip of your tongue. I think you know what I am speaking of. You feel as though it is your duty to respond and to respond quickly.

It is not your duty to respond quickly. It may not even be your duty to respond at all. Therefore, I have a suggestion: Do not offer quick answers. Do not be the one who speaks first, but be proud to be the one who speaks last; especially if you have the last word, you shall have been the one who has made the greater impression.

The last word is the more potent if it is but a word. The fewer words spoken, the greater their impact. Certainly, those who babble on, even if they have many good thoughts to share, will eventually cover their own ideas with their own verbiage. Therefore, to obey my own rule, I shall be brief. In a nutshell, it is this: *the greater power is that which is contained, rather than that which is simply strewn about.*

Thoughts, when they are contained, will give birth to words and actions of considerable focus, great thrust and ultimately great effect. Therefore, if you would be more effectual and more effective, be more guarded and wait until you have considered the matter before you express an opinion. And even if you have a ready opinion, hesitate a moment to consider whether it is the best time to express it, and whether or not you'd have been better off to have said nothing. For very often, nothing is your best response.

You have not been provided with this in your culture: that is, the permission to say nothing. You've been taught that you are duty-bound and obliged to always give an answer, even to a fool. I've seen it so many times, that you will give a fool of your time and of your energy. Moreover, you will waste your pearls of wisdom. And therefore when you have come to an opportunity to share them, you have little left, for you will have wasted your good things on fools.

So I say to you that sometimes the best response is no response. And when you have broken that slavery to a custom, you will no longer feel as though politeness requires you to answer fools. You will be free, and you will thank me, I think, in that moment.

NAMES

You have power in your names. There is power in all names. The meaning of all things is to be found in the name. Meditate upon this.

Would you know the goodness of a thing, the rightness of a thing, the use of a thing? Would you unravel a mystery? Intone the name. Speak it. Intone it. Meditate upon it. Write it over and over and over and over until the thought you are awaiting comes to you.

You are looking for the hidden meaning behind the outer vibration. The outer vibration is the name. The inner vibration is the reality of the experience of what is named or described by your words. That is why Eastern mystics are addicted to chanting. They chant anything and everything to know what is behind it. And when they have found the things they wish to manifest, they chant them over and over again.

But you need not chant in Oriental languages. There is nothing about these languages that gives them greater power than your own. They have the advantage of being native. Chinese do not chant in Japanese. And Japanese do not chant in Hindu. Why should you chant in any of these languages?

If all Easterners chant in their own languages, you should chant in yours. What is true of the Easterner to himself in his own time and place ought to be true for the Westerner. But you see, Westerners adopt the outward customs of the East without understanding why they are what they are.

Some of your old chants are called psalms. Some are short and some are long, but other verses may do as well. It need not be a poem that you chant. It may simply be an idea clearly expressed.

Work with what I have given you, and you will be most happy and satisfied.

KNOTS

Some of you are very good bead stringers, yes? Some of you are good knitters, crocheters and sewers. You put prayer into the things that you make for people, and these prayers will be turned into healing energy.

Do you know, my friends, that the weaver's art was always a mystical one for this reason: every time a knot is tied, it is said, a promise is made. And every time a knot is broken a promise is undone. That is why it can be very unlucky to have your beads break. So you will use very good string, and you will make very good knots, and you will make a prayer with every knot.

Some, who work wickedness, make a curse with every knot, can you imagine? But you will make a prayer with every knot, and you will wear it yourself or give it away. With every stitch or every knot, whether you are weaving or sewing or knitting or crocheting, it is the same. This is magic, and there is power in it.

You can make yourself magical beads of protection. If you tie spells into them, they will work for you. We do this in the East. It is the origin of your rosary beads. This is something everyone can do. We spirits also believe that a power that is brought into these knots is locked into the article, and so resides therein, not to be lost. I will teach you many mystical practices and tell you stories of these things, sometimes. You have heard of a sortilege? It is a string with knots in it. A rosary is a sortilege.

Let me tell you a story now, for interest's sake, for knots are very difficult things. When the great Alexander came to the borders of the Persian empire, he was presented with something that was called the Gordian knot. And it was a great knot, for it was said that any who could undo it would rule the East. So Alexander looked at it, and it being a very tough knot indeed, he drew his sword and with a single stroke cleaved it in half. Therefore, if you find any knots that bind you, don't bother to unravel them. Cut them, for that is one of the best ways to undo a knot. To break a spell, we break the knot. We don't untie it. We cut it. For what has been broken can never be put back.

Some have asked: how do we do this with the effects our parents have had on us? Cut the knot; cut the cord; sever the relationship if you are brave. It is hard to unravel. Some have spent all their lives, much money and psychoanalysis, and have not undone the knot...which a single stroke of a blade might better have undone. I mean that symbolically, of course. Sever the connection. That is the best way to break a spell...to cut it. Alexander knew this well. The spell is there as long as the connection is not severed. For even when the knot is undone, the remains of the knot, the remembrance of the knot, remains in the pattern of the string. Do you understand?

Cut the knot. That is my recommendation.

BLOCKS

As you are working so hard, my friends, you think, "Oh, my, my, my, my...I am working so hard. I am so lonely in my hard work." But that is because you are forgetting that "The Lord helps those who help themselves." So if you are helping yourself, the Lord is helping you, too, only you don't see it; you don't know it, but it is happening. You are so caught up in the work that you are doing, you forget that there is something else going on in the universe around you.

Now sometimes you may say, "Well, the harder I work, the greater are the obstacles. It almost seems as if the work is working against me." Therefore, ask yourself next time you find obstacles, whether or not these obstacles are indeed meant to prevent you from going any further in one direction so that you will be forced to take a new direction. Sometimes an obstacle is like a detour placed in your path because it is not advisable for you to go further in that direction. It is time for you to make a turn to the left or to the right, and so a barrier is placed in your way.

Now sometimes it is not such a high barrier, so you are only asked to step over it. It is a thing of no great consequence. It is in the nature of climbing and going into new territory that one sometimes has to step over rocks, and the path, not having been walked before, must be cleared. In the process of clearing it you cannot expect it to be smooth, but that there will be bumps and lumps and occasionally, I suppose, you will have to ford a stream. But that is expected. When you go hiking in the wilderness, you do not expect it to be like a superhighway. You would be disappointed if it was such. You want to climb over things. You like the exercise... the challenge. That is why some people climb mountains.

Well then, there are also other things which are going on. For as you have to climb over a barrier, it is not your power alone which takes you over it. *Every step along the way, there is help for you.*

Now many of you have found in your lives that you have some big hurdles to overcome, but you know that there is power there for you to help you to do it. And by reaching out to that power, you do grow in strength, and you are able to feel, later, something that is very important. You have felt the power of God with you, working with you. Had you never come to that barrier or that hurdle, you would never have had to rely upon a Higher Power than your own, because you would not have needed it.

So, it often happens that in learning about one's Higher

Power or God, that one has to learn it through encountering hurdles and barriers. Because then they must make that special effort that they're not capable of doing on their own. And for this reason, barriers exist.

Now once the barrier has been overcome through Divine assistance, one has gained a great deal of knowledge in that the same obstacle will no longer be encountered, although others will be, depending upon what lessons have to be learned. But one does not have to learn the same lesson twice. Indeed, having learned the lesson, you are filled with a great sense of power, not only your own power, but God power, because you have worked with this power. The creative energy is now flowing into you, and you have something to give others who are facing similar barriers, who are facing similar challenges.

My friends, there is no obstacle, there is no barrier set in front of you which you cannot confront. But it is first important to consult to see whether it is there to redirect you or whether it is there for you to step over. That is important for you to know. How can you know which it is? Then it is good for you to refer to your Higher Power, to your consciousness which is divine...and say, "Show me a sign. If this barrier is one which is a detour showing me a new way to go, I will accept it. But if it is meant for me to climb through this, renew in me the courage and the desire to overcome whatever it is that challenges me."

Now, one way that we do come to know a hurdle, as opposed to a barrier, is to learn to distinguish the difference between them. And I would say that a barrier is that by which one will be redirected and a hurdle is something which one will have to go over, to persist and thereby become stronger by doing it. A hurdle has about it something which is conquerable, something which shows itself not to be a barrier but merely something to get past. Whereas a barrier seems insurmountable and indeed probably is insurmountable or should be left in place.

The hurdle is never too high for you to climb, though sometimes when you come to it, you may say, "I am feeling weak. I am not feeling strong enough to get over it. It is not that it is so high but that I am so weak." And at that point you must try. You must try to give it your best energy and ask God to help you. And if you do, you will succeed because you are going to become stronger than you know you are. By yourself you are nothing, but in collaboration with this Divine Power...I tell you, you will come over these hurdles because they are put there so you can do just exactly that.

If you come to a barrier, then say, "Show me the way that

I must go now. If this means no further, I accept that. I accept that God has placed something in my way that says, "Stop; do not persist," and then look to every other direction for an opening...that which shows itself to be the new direction, the new path, and you will not be disappointed. You will be shown a new way.

You are never in a box. You will never come to a dead end. There is just a detour and you will see that when you have not enough sense to know when to change your path, then Divine Providence provides a barrier that forces you to look in a new direction.

I hope that you will give some thought to these things.

ACTION

When you move, Spirit can help you to move, but if you sit still, what can Spirit do?

You understand that Spirit can guide a moving hand, but not a hand that is still. And I say this to you, my friends, *if you are moving, you are easy to guide,* but if you are frozen, if you are sitting still, it is very hard to get you up and move you about.

Now, I must tell you something. Many of you sit and think and think and think and try to have all the answers before you come to the moment where the answers would be put to use. You try to plan. Sometimes in your meditations you ask Spirit to give you everything you need to know, not only for the day but for the week, the month, the year. Perhaps Spirit should give you your whole life in a book and then you would not have to think, you would only read each page. But you see, it is not like that, not at all...no, no.

It is so important to come to each step and to be open to guidance. You could not possibly understand if we were to tell you the events that may be coming for you six months from now. You could not possibly see how they would relate to your present situation. Perhaps they would seem disconnected from everything that you are doing now. And for this reason, some of you who like to have psychic readings, afterwards consider them so strange. Or when Spirit gives you a message for something in the future, you think Spirit could not possibly be right, for it speaks of things that seem so far from where you are now. But there will be many changes as you go through life, and you will find that by a curious set of circumstances you are often led to some totally new endeavor.

You need only look into your past to see the truth of what I am saying. Because, of course, isn't it so that you have had a very curious path thus far? Maybe you forget how remarkable your lives have been. Maybe it is because you are so caught up in the questions of today that you have failed to realize that your lives have been a series of most interesting, if not to say remarkable, meetings. You've kept appointments with your destiny. You've made changes. Some of the changes seemed almost as if they were forced upon you. But if you will examine further, you will see that you have found yourself confronted with a new understanding and had to, of course, act accordingly.

Why, if you look back at your life, you will see that some of the most important moments could not have been planned, were not planned...they simply happened. And what made them important was that they were not so much of and by themselves important, but that you understood they were and acted accordingly.

Of course, that is what is meant by "taking advantage of an opportunity". For opportunities come and go, but it is those which you act upon that have meaning in your life.

Now I say to you this: if you will be a bit more adventuresome and not feel as though you have to have everything made clear before you, you will be a lot better off. You will not travel with so much mental baggage... yes, mental baggage. Mental baggage becomes to the spirit something very burdensome indeed. And the spirit somehow is constrained by all of this knowledge which it has had before the fact, and sometimes is prevented from gaining the knowledge which is part of the moment.

Now, I offer this thought: I would like to suggest to you that you be prepared to change your whole life's course at a moment, if it were shown to you that it were a wiser thing to do. If a truth became apparent to you which you had not understood before, would you be willing to change? That is a question which you must ask yourself. But I think if you are free, you could say yes. And if you are not free, you could not say yes. And until you are able to say yes, whatever it is that makes you say no is the thing which is holding you.

Many of you at this moment are sitting right on the fence. You are half changed and half not changed. It is a very anxious state. Well, the fact is that if you are any changed, you are completely changed. It only appears that part of you has yet to finish changing.

Believe it when I say to you that whatever consciousness you possess, whatever awareness you have, they are sufficient for today's actions and today's need. The rest will come in good time.

Bless you.

GETTING AND SPENDING

There was a poet whose name was Wordsworth...one might ponder that name for awhile. He said something about "Getting and spending we lay waste our powers..." The process of acquiring and disbursement, yes? You lay waste your powers.

What are your powers? Your powers are absorbed by this process which might better be put into creative work. But it seems necessary to get and to spend. I have a suggestion. The more you spend, the more you must get. If you see that in spending much, one must devote one's self to getting much, you will see that if one spends less, one will need to get a little less, and perhaps use one's powers for other things. Now he did not say what would come of the use of these powers, were they put somewhere else. He did not say whether one might get something from the use of these powers, but he implied it. Because power that is dissipated in one place and put to use in another may earn differently; may be used differently.

We observe that many of you have a great deal of power which is being used, shall we say, ineffectually. You are not getting the greatest rewards for your efforts. And perhaps you are laying waste your powers, even in spending. Even in disbursement one is putting out energy. It takes a lot of energy to spend money, yes?

It's the energy you're not aware of that you have to think about. But where would you put your power if you did not put it into these things? What would you do with it that is more productive? That is the question. And if you know a place that would be more productive, would you not want it there? If you use your powers and your gifts optimally, if you put them in the best possible direction, will you not make the greatest profit? Then perhaps one can only re-examine how he or she is expending energy and redirect it to the new way, thinking less in terms of getting and spending, and more in terms of utilization. Because sooner or later power must be channeled, and it must be used. There is no point in having it if one does not use it. But it is in the idea of getting and spending rather than the idea of utilizing that I think one loses the track.

You've all come here with something to utilize, and you are refreshed in that. If you use it, you do not run out of it. You are given more. Where are your powers coming from anyway? Do your powers come from getting? Or spending? Neither. Your powers are gifts. And if you use them, you get more of them. But you know the force does not give unwisely.

And if you do not use them well, you are not given more until you do. Do I make sense to you? Because I think this poet, Wordsworth, was alluding to something more than things of this world: to take some source from here and to spend it there, to get and to spend, is only moving around what is, not using these powers in a new way. And to lay waste the powers does not mean to expend them, but rather to ignore them. For that is the true message: you expend no power that is creative. You lay waste its power because you do not utilize it. It is ignored for that other activity, which is only to take from here and bring to there.

For this I invite you all to meditate upon the nature of your powers, your psychic and spiritual and physical powers, and to fight to express them, and you will not have to worry about getting and spending. That will be taken care of because these powers will bring you all that is needed, instead of being confined to being merchants.

You will understand, I am certain.

ENVIRONMENT

When we use the word environment today, for many people it means ecology. It means establishing a balance between nature and man. I would like to bring it a little closer to home. I would like to speak about the environment which is closest to you...the one you live in, your home.

Now I wonder as I say the word "home" how many of you feel as though the place where you live is a home? For some, it may only seem to be a temporary housing, a shell which will be shed sometime. Perhaps ultimately it is so, for all homes and all houses will have to be surrendered when one goes to the next life. And even so, it is probable that each of you will have additional homes in your lives. But, you know, many people do nothing about their environment when it is not an ideal one to begin with. Such persons will say, "Well, this is only temporary. There is no reason to put any energy into this. I do not own it. I only rent it. There is no purpose for me to concern myself with this because I will not be here long." But I say to you, if you stay there any time at all, it will have an effect on you.

If the space that you live in feels like a home, then it can do for you what a home can do. But if it does not feel like a home, how can it provide you with a home feeling? If the space you live in, even if it is one room, resonates to your vibration, has in it things that are strongly like you or complement you, if the space is organized in such a way that it pleases you or serves you well and if you fit comfortably into it, then you and your space are in harmony, and you will function as a person who has a good home base. But if you are out of harmony with your house, if you feel like a stranger in a borrowed space, you will be in some ways a naked person, a person who has no shell, a person who has no small environment to call their own.

Now it is true that some holy men have said that the world is their environment, who wear only simple garments and who sleep out of doors or in the home of anyone who takes them in...I think that, for certain individuals, that is possible. It takes a great sense of freedom from this material world to be able to do that. But if you have not yet arrived at this stage, do not be unhappy. For it is only a very few, and by their choice, that decide it is better for them to have no specific place, but to have the greater space...and therefore they are free.

Most people do not wish to be that free. Most people wish to have a sense of belonging, and therefore the things they surround themselves with are called belongings. And they are belonging as much to their belongings as their belongings belong to them. And this is not bad, as long as what they acquire is truly right for them, and fits and harmonizes with them. Then one may even say that it adds. But if, in fact, it is not useful, if it is something that is extraneous, then we can say that by its presence, it subtracts. What does it subtract? It subtracts space. It takes away the amount of free space which might be better occupied by something that reflects you.

As you live in a space, whether your space is very small or very large...it does not matter, because you will learn some lessons by living in a small space: how, with economy of means, to get the most from very little. At other times when you are blessed with a larger space, you will have the task of balancing and arranging it so that you can control it, without it controlling you. As you work on your space, your space works on you. As I have said, when it is perfectly in harmony with you, it can provide you with so many things. It is for this reason that so much money, time, effort and energy is put into taking care of one's home and decorating it.

To many people the word decoration or interior decoration merely means to put some cosmetic application to this space, but it is much more important. It is a fundamental organization of space, arrangement of space and utilization of space. It is a fundamental design of color, form...and as much as what is there, what isn't there is important also. And when all these things work, you work. And when these things are in conflict with each other, you will find that you do not enjoy being in your space. It does not feel like a home to you, and you are somehow an orphan.

It is essential, I say, for you to take control of your space, your environment and to put your mark upon it...but to do it in such a way that it is not arbitrary, but truly a reflection of your life and your personality...to do this a little at a time, so that eventually, as you change, your space is constantly reflecting you and it is a true home.

Because the home is the extension of one who lives in it; it may change and it may move just as you may. And you may transfer this understanding which you have achieved in one place to another.

DECEPTION

Deception is a deep subject. To discuss it, we might be here a long time. Well, let's face it, we *are* here a long time, so we might as well use it wisely. What better way to use our time than to speak about such things, yes? Better to speak of them first, than to experience them and speak of them later.

To begin with, a person or a spirit which is self serving is one you must always be aware of, whether that being is in human form or speaks from the spirit realms. What I mean by a self-serving spirit is one who uses others to further his own ends. You may remember in your Judeo-Christian Bible that there are many times when the God of the Old and New Testaments speaks to the prophets, telling them to do this and that and so on. But you will observe that this God is speaking for the good of mankind, not for the good of God. God is not interested in furthering God's particular needs, God having no specific needs in this instance. God's need is rather that mankind be better, that the human race be better off through the advancement of truth and justice, that the righteous be victorious and so on. Therefore this God says to certain prophets: These things shall you do, observe and so on.

The Ten Commandments may seem to some to show a very jealous God who is self-serving ("Have no other gods before me ..."). But this God is saying, "Listen, I am your friend. I am here for you. If you go to this one and that one and another, you will only confuse yourselves. I am here for you." It is not that this God or Creator is jealous, it's that this God says, "Have your priority first with Me, for I am the One who empowers you and gives to you. I am helpful to you, and this is for your good."

Now I mention this because, after all, this is your Ultimate Spirit. In each culture there is such a spirit. It is always the same one in the end, but it is called by many, many names in many cultures. It speaks every language. It comes in many different disguises. It speaks through many kinds of mediums and prophets. For what are the gods of other religions if not manifestations, representatives and emissaries of the Ultimate Spirit. It is all very much the same and in this one sees something rather clearly. One sees that in all of this, it is the well-being and the good for all that is being served, not the vanity or ego of any. It is no one being profited at anyone else's expense. It is not God being a big shot. It is God performing as good, the good, the universal good.

Now let us look for a moment at what you call evil...the devil...Satan, and all the rest you know by these names. There are many names for negative force and negative energy. This is the force that wants to be served, that wants to enslave, that says, "You will serve me. I am your master. You are my slave."

Whereas the good says, "Serve as a servant, not as a slave. Do because you love to do, because you want to do, because you choose to do. And if you do not choose to do, it is well." We, positive spirits, are patient to wait until you come to your own choices, but not so evil.

Evil says, "If you do not do it, I will force you. I will make you. I will insist." Or it will try to persuade you by flattery, appealing to some instinct other than a noble one and so on and so forth, perhaps, trying to use power to coerce.

So we see that between good and evil there is a different approach: one is to help, to advise, to allow, and whatsoever is given is not something which is required so much as it is offered. But that which is evil, also deceives. It uses not the truth, but the untruth. It promises things which it cannot deliver. And what's more, it somehow misleads in order to profit itself. So in terms of deception, my friends, you will see that that which seeks to serve the greater good will never seek to deceive. Sometimes people will misunderstand and perhaps delude themselves, but in the end truth is nothing that is deceptive.

Evil, on the other hand, inevitably is deceptive, for often it poses at being good, which in its very nature is deceptive, for it means one thing, but says another. It does not want to tell you what it really desires, and so it makes some pretense. It creates a fabrication in order to string you along...do you understand ?...to involve you...never mind that you will one day find out that this is not real. For the time you are deceived, you have been had, and that is long enough to suit its purposes. So it is calculated on the part of evil, interestingly enough, that sooner or later it will be discovered. Sooner or later the deception will be found out, but it will have accomplished its end, which was to have you for a little while, because evil knows it can never keep you forever. Evil knows it will ultimately lose to good, for good is Truth, and it will ultimately give way to Truth, as darkness must give way to the light. So deception is the technique by which evil gets its little way in this world for awhile.

The purpose of spirit, whether it be God or the angels working for God, is to be helpful and not enslave man but rather liberate man. Not to tie people, but to free people. Therefore, I ask you to observe that some religions, who claim to be the true religions of this God, tie people to them rather than free people from fear. They tie people by fear. You've seen this. Now I will tell you something...that sometimes, the best practice of goodness, or God's will (which is nothing

but the same: goodness and God's will are the same thing)...
may be observed as what you call Christian practice, which
is nothing more than the practice of goodness.

Christian practice is practiced by all good people, whether
they have ever heard of Jesus or not. It does not make it
Christian because it has Jesus's name attached to it. We have
had Christians long before Jesus. We have had Christians in
every faith, because they practiced the spirit of Christ. One
manifestation of the spirit of the Christ is Jesus and another is
Our Lord Buddha...call it Buddhism or Christianity. It's the
same thing. We, in the East, say "one who has the Buddha
enlightenment." It's the same thing...the point being this,
that these great teachers, or avatars, from whom the spirit
emanated into this world, were the great liberators. They freed
people from the fear and tyranny of religion and oppression
and guilt and all of these horrible things. They helped to
free them from karma, because they gave them the tools to
overcome. They gave them the lessons by which they could
become spiritually evolved, make contact with their creative
force, God (Higher Power), in whatever shape or form their
culture knew God to be, and, to become true children of that
spiritual force. Every one of these teachers was trying to put
the power into the hands of each and every person, and to
take it away from the Pharisees or from the establishment.
They were all anti-establishment, in terms of the spirit. They

did not, however, advocate anarchy. They advocated a form of spiritual self-involvement.

The reason I say all of this is if you want to see deception at work, then you need only to see those who claim to speak the Christian word but who do not speak it. They enslave through fear rather than liberate through the sense of giving each person some power, some integrity and some sense of well-being. This is also the case with Buddhism, which is filled with mispractice, as well as Judaism and every religion. There is always the mispractice of some priests who enslave by fear and create dependency to have power for themselves, for they are egotists or greedy or both, and they are treating the world as if they are all children, which to a degree is true.

People are children. But the true teacher says, "Children, you must grow up. And I will help you to grow up. I am your friend...your spiritual parent." But the false teacher is the one who seeks to become the authoritarian, who does not let the children grow, who keeps the children small, stunted, dependent. That is not in the spirit of light; that is not in the spirit of truth; that is deceptive. To discern this, all one has to do is look at the basic teaching.

You may remember that some several hundred years ago the sacred book, the Bible, the one by which all your Western

Judeo-Christian religions are kept, was never allowed in the ordinary person's hands. Even when it was printed, and never mind those that were copied by hand and precious... they were shown only one page at a time, so that no one could read and look around and get ideas about what these words meant. It was not permitted that the ordinary person should have a chance to think about this holy work.

Then there came a very powerful king in England named James I. He said that he felt the greatest mistake in his whole life was to have the Bible translated into the English language and be sold and distributed to anybody who wanted it. Because out of that came the Reformation in England, and instead of one religion, they had fifty. On every street corner somebody was standing up saying, "This is what it is all about..." The strange thing and the irony is that each one of these new preachers was just as limited and deceptive as the ones who had gone before. It was simply one brand of limited viewpoint as opposed to another. And they would argue and say, "This is what it means. That is what it means," and from it form new religions.

There is this deceptive practice, then, which comes about when one thinks that because they have the work in their hand that they are also possessed with the power to make it understandable for others, or to somehow define for others the limitation, the breadth or the depth of it.

Only a fool thinks he knows something for certain. A wise man knows nothing is for certain. He hopes some things are, but he knows little is, other than the fact that good ultimately is there in one shape or form or another.

I hope this will be helpful to you.

RECOVERY

Recovery is a very important word. It is a very important concept, and it is a very important process.

Life is all about this wonderful word: recovery.

You start and you begin to go forward and you falter and in order to go forward again, you must recover. You must recover your balance. If you find you have fallen, you must stand up again. If you find you have gone in the wrong direction, you must turn around and re-direct yourself. If you find that you have behaved in a way which has been counterproductive, you need to amend that behavior. And this process of recovery is the one that gives you the greatest sense of accomplishment.

It is very easy to achieve your goals if there are no obstacles and the wind is at your back. Believe me, there is a certain thrill of exhilaration as you move forward carried by the wind. But the greatest sense of accomplishment, my friends, is that which comes when the wind is at your face, and you must struggle, falter and recover. For in that moment, you have truly triumphed over those things that have perhaps too long defeated you.

The person who is, for example, chained to some old habit, and in the moment realizes this old habit is asserting itself, says: "Ah, me, my old ways compel me forward. I am a helpless victim of my habits," is a person who feels very horrible about himself or herself, has a sense of powerlessness and a certain sense of defeat.

Recovery begins when such a person says: "Ah, me, my old ways assert themselves again. But wait...I will desist, for this moment I will not let the momentum of my past carry me forward. I will take an individual and decisive step. For this moment I will simply not do what I have done before under these circumstances." And in this case, the pattern of habit may be broken for a moment. But since one does not wish to remain motionless forever, frozen in the state of non-doing for fear that one's actions are going to be wrong, one needs a plan of recovery to supplement wrong action or inappropriate action with right action.

I think, for example, of the ones who are eating food that is unhealthy, the junk food which is not good for them and they know it. And all the time they are eating it they know it is not good for them, even though it tastes very good and they are addicted to it. But one day they say, "Wait, I am eating something that is not good for me," and take not one bite more but put down this food. In that moment, recovery has begun. In that moment it is not enough to stop eating; they need to eat correctly and to amend their behavior.

So, you are ready to recover. You give up this way for a way which you gladly embrace. You then choose something that is right and appropriate for you and proceed to eat that. Now you have two important events to observe. For one, you feel empowered that you have stopped the old behavior. Secondly, you feel proud of yourself that you have commenced right action. You have taken a step for recovery. You have not solved your whole life's problem. You have not corrected all of your behavior. You have taken care of one thing.

There is a sense of triumph that comes in that moment. Look back over your life and see how many things you have conquered in your life. You have conquered them really one moment at a time. And they have truly been victories. Those are the hardest things in life and yet the most gratifying.

Did you ever wonder if perhaps you have some negative behavior so that you may have the opportunity for such triumph and success? Indeed, it may exist in you so that you are challenged by it, that you may grow because of it.

And so this process of recovery is not a single fixed goal, but it is a constant returning to that awareness and right action, even if after awhile you, who have given up junk food for a day, find yourself on another day eating it again. Yet you must stop and say to yourself, "It is not enough that I stop once. I must repeat this action. I must repeat this action over and over again." Just as one must repeat all good actions. It is not enough to say, "I did a good thing once. I was kind once. Oh, several times I was honest. Oh, from time to time I take a look at myself and do a personal inventory." No, no... right action must be done over and over again; appropriate right action. And it is nothing if you think of it as something which is done once and that is final and fixed, and that you have done it and it needs to be done no more. *Recovery is like bathing. It needs to be done daily.*

One constantly has to get back in the centered position, constantly return to that which is the highest and constantly attune oneself. It is like a violin player. He spends a great deal of time tuning his violin. He does not just tune it and then play it. He must keep tuning it because it goes out of tune. And when he hears it go out of tune, that is the time to tune it. And so it is with you. For a thing may start to fall apart, but if you catch it in time, if you act in time, all is not lost. There is no disaster. There is no great crisis. But even when there is a great crisis, you have seen so many times that out of every pile of ashes arises a Phoenix bird; that there is recovery even in disaster. Those which seem to be the most annihilating of life experiences sometimes give birth to a whole new state of consciousness. And perhaps they are precipitated by a great need within the individual to have a personal transformation which is radical. Perhaps it is the ego which needs a very strong knock.

Whatever is the case, it does not matter except to know that life is about getting back into that place of centeredness and connectedness, and that is a continual, ongoing process, and there is no need to fear that something is lost, because in recovery you get it back. Not only do you get what you lost but something you hadn't, which is the knowledge of how it is to be secure in what you are doing.

Many people have certain things that they are comfortable about because they do not understand them. And when they are suddenly deprived of them, when they have lost the ability to function in a certain way, they are beside themselves. They don't know what happened. They don't understand the loss, because they never understood how it was that they did what they did, or had what they had in the first place.

Sometimes life and the universe deprive you of a thing, not that you must forever be without it, but for just a little while that you must lose it to regain it. Then you will understand how it is you come by it and how you may keep it. So sometimes a thing is taken away for a little while so that you will go through the process of recovering it.

Therefore, I bring up the subject of recovery because many people do not understand why errors occur. Often they occur for the purpose of providing means to recover. Because recovery is a process of learning, and that is the thing that most people don't understand. They see it as a penitence or atonement or as some kind of unpleasant remedy. But a remedy is a blessing. A remedy is also a lesson because all of it, after all, is learning how to live better.

That is the secret of life: learning how to live better. And better means in the fullest sense of that word, to improve all aspects of living: their sense of the moment enlarges and becomes greater than that which is small, in front of their nose, and their sense of involvement becomes truly extended to a large awareness of now.

FULFILLMENT

When you feel a lack of fulfillment in your life, it is because you expect more of you than God expects from you. That was always the devil's trouble. The devil always wanted more than God wanted; more and different. That is everyone's devil, not only Satan, but the devil of all religion is that what was enough for God was not enough for Adam and Eve. What was enough was never enough, because, you see, God is satisfied and the devil is not. That which is negative is never enough. It always negates that which is positive.

Perhaps when you learn to be satisfied, you will not have such a difficult time in accepting yourself. You will be satisfied with what you are and realize that although you may be something different tomorrow, what you are today is quite good. You can always be better, but that gives you something to look forward to. What will be a year from now will, of course, be very different than what is today, but then that shall be something for a year away, not for today. What is for today is for today, and that is good enough. But what is for a year from now is not for today, and today is not for then. Today is for today, and then is for then.

So love today and love then when then has come. Another

way of saying this is: enjoy the fruits of the season. Those who pick apples before their time will find them green and not to their liking. Those who come too late will find them rotten and fallen on the ground. The secret of life is to come in time—not before and not after—to love a thing for what it is. And if the apples be green, then enjoy what other fruits be ripe. Does that make sense?

It is not so hard to live and be fulfilled. You must let go. If your way is the best way, then you have no problems. But if your way is not the best way and you have problems, let go of your way. Try another way. I have always said that as long as one's way is the best way, then hold on to it. But when one finds his or her way is not the best way, then one should let go of it. You see, by letting go of your way, you will find another way. I shall speak more specifically to this point.

Well, you see, it begins with a way of thinking. Actions are only an extension of thought; you know that. So we don't deal with the action, per se, we'll deal with the thought. It begins in *expectation*—that you have an idea of what is good, that you think you know what God wants, or what is good, or what better is.

What is good for God may not be your way of thinking. What you think is the right direction—what seems to be the right direction—might not be the right direction at all. It is just possible, though improbable, that God would prefer that you sit in a chair and think for three days and not leave it except to relieve yourself of other pressures. But you have another agenda. You have the agenda that you have decided is the way you must conduct your affairs. You have your business. You have things to do. You cannot simply sit around and be obedient to God's will. You have to be about your business, and therein comes the rub. There is the conflict. You will find out what I am saying.

Now if you were to surrender totally, you would say that if it suited God, you would do business. But, if it did not suit God, you would not do business. If it suited God that you pack your bags and travel halfway around the world to a strange place you had never been before and to leave all else behind you, you would do it. But few would be willing.

Now God is a very wise God and does not ask you to do something that would seem crazy because then you would doubt your sanity and doubt the sanity of the God who asks it. So God asks in a more subtle way to have you turn loose your grip. God asks you to think a little differently every day—a little differently, and to act a little differently, not a lot differently, a little, just a little. But a little, by a little, by a little. Not a mile a day, but an inch a day. And all of a sudden you are in a new space, and you are doing things differently, and you are feeling differently.

Your grip is being loosened one finger at a time. But you are having to at least let one finger go, and not to struggle too hard. You are burning up a lot of energy struggling. Some people have said, "What have you got to lose?" And you could say, "I've got everything to lose." But, if you have everything to lose then you must have everything to gain. Because you cannot lose everything without gaining everything. That is a law, not only of metaphysics, but of physics: the law of displacement. If you lose one thing, you'll gain another. So he who loses all, gains all.

But you have your ways; each of you has your ways. Ask yourself if your ways are God's ways. And if you say, "Well, God's ways are not tested. I do not know where they will take me," they cannot take you in a bad direction. For God is good—the collective good—and does not intend a life of misery for you, but a life of happiness, even if happiness means leaving your way behind and all the things that go with your way. That is very difficult for some.

You may remember that Jesus told the Disciples to go and sell everything they had, give it to the poor and to follow Him. I do not think that any of them regretted this action. I do not think that had they remained in the fish business or whatever, they would have been happier. I think history bears that out, that although there were many difficult moments, they certainly went from very ordinary lives to very great ones. And so it has been proven through all your saints. Perhaps Saint Francis, leaving behind all his earthly wealth to serve God; he had a choice and he never regretted it. Buddha and many of our great incarnate Masters of the East were the same. Why, I ask you time and time again, have the great Masters always said: "The only freedom is to be able to set aside our way for the Divine way."?

We are prisoners of our own systems, our own thought patterns. That makes us prisoners. But we must be guided by something, otherwise we will wander aimlessly, and we will be fruitless. Therefore, we can only be guided by a greater consciousness for good, and yet maintain our freedom from the traps which our own systems inevitably place us in. Does that make sense?

This will give you something to ponder.

MYTHOLOGY

For those of you who have grown up and suffered from having had a difficult family member, I offer the following ideas. Let us say, for instance, that that person was your mother, although we might well be talking about your father or sister or brother or so on, as the case may be. But let us just say mother for the time being, and you will know how to fill in the appropriate person.

Well, suppose your mother, having earned your poor opinion over the years by being cruel, negative and causing pain, were to have a miraculous reformation of character, would you not be the first to embrace this? Would you not be willing to let bygones be bygones and forgive her if she would, in fact, live in such a reformed manner?

Now realistically speaking, for some people there is little hope of that. However, the point I'm trying to make is that it's not that you hold any vendetta against your mother. Were she to reform herself, you would be the first to acknowledge that. It is that she is unrepentant and unreformed in her behavior; not willing to accept responsibility for her actions, and proud and haughty at the same time, that make her so intolerable. So why should you put up with a judgmental, pompous, arrogant and grandiose woman?

Suppose that troublesome person is a daffy sister: what is she to you that you owe putting up with her craziness? Nothing, really, because she does not function in the capacity of sister. So noticing this you have killed the myth of sisterhood, just as in the other case you have killed the myth of motherhood. That is what you have slain: the mythological mother, the mythological sister, etc., and now you are simply dealing with people on a real basis. You have stopped giving people a special role in your life which they've disrespected as such. So, welcome to enlightenment. That is what life is about. Seeing people as they truly are to you.

Many people go around with a mythological belief in the American dream, the American family, motherhood, sisterhood, brotherhood, fatherhood, childhood. People have these beliefs all the time. They have children and they watch television with these happy little family shows, then their own children turn out to be monsters, take drugs and destroy the house...they wonder what happened to them. They can't understand why it's not like the TV or the movies or the magazines.

My friends, you create reality, not mythology. You may believe in mythology, which many people do, but you have overcome that mythology. You have entered behind the veil. You have entered the real. You know what you are dealing with and that's very mature of you. It's already changing your life.

Now, I've a suggestion: once you've crossed this threshold and respected the situation in which you find yourself, you must bury the hatchet. Once it has cut the cord you need not bring it out time after time, making little chops all over the place. Let it go and move on from mother or father or sister, etc. They've served their time and now you must let go. Why take them to bed every night in your thoughts and wake up with them in the morning? Let's put them out of mind and get on with the business of living. For otherwise, your old tapes take you over and over the past but they do not take you forward. What you know, you know. You don't need to know it twenty times over.

Life has both comfort and newness, which some people call discomfort. The comfort, and that which is familiar to you are something which you need to have always centrally in your life. But, in time, you change what is comfortable to you. Little by little you expand your horizons, your capabilities; you change and evolve so that what is comfortable for you today was not so comfortable to you many years ago. You grow to become responsible for who you are and who you have become: your actions, your opinions, your desires and so on and so forth. You have now become whole by being perfectly yourself. You are not driven by past myths about who you should be or who others must be to be around you. You have accepted situations as they are and no longer need to be a slave to someone else's tyranny or their mythology. And that, my friends, is what we call freedom.

Bless you and all your hard work.

DESIRE

Desire, temptation, need...these come into your mind and form the basis of compulsion; for what else is compulsion? It is something which overwhelms the mind.

There are many thoughts that come and go in this world where you live. Some are clean and some are unclean. Some are lewd and some are wicked, and they all come to you... the good, the bad and the indifferent. The clean and unclean thoughts come to you altogether, just like life in the street is simultaneous: the good, the bad and the indifferent. You will never be able to avoid this. Therefore, the great karma and the great challenge is to discern the good, the bad and the indifferent, and to let the unclean thought, the bad thought, the compulsive thought, the desire thought pass through you. *Do not resist it*, for it will then engage you in a battle and make you its prisoner by having wars with you.

No, do not resist it. Do not even pay attention to it. Ignore it. Let it pass through you. Do not resist it but do not take it up. Do not entertain it. Do not play with it, consider it, give it space; and if necessary, to push it away, entertain a thought of your own choosing to replace it. Dislodge it by reaching to a thought that is good.

I am saying, to entertain thoughts which will push these things away will, in fact, help you not to become their prisoners. For if you take them up, they will possess you and they will control you. But, likewise, they will control those of you who run from them...never run from them. Do not be afraid of any thought. You are strong enough not to resist, but not to take it up...for it cannot possess you unless you take it. So let it go by you.

Now this you will have to consider moment by moment. Because just when you have let one pass, another may come. And if this is so, if there are many coming to you, know that it is because your mind is too vacant. You need to put your mind to work actively in things which are important. Because a vacant mind invites unclean thoughts.

I am not confusing this with meditation, but I am saying there are times when you are vulnerable, and in those moments you need to put your mind to work on things that are positive and useful. But do not run fearfully from negativity. Do not think that you can ever find a safe haven from negative thoughts, fears, doubts and all manner of seductions because, my friends, they are always around. You are never too old to be seduced. You are never too old to be tempted, and you are never too old not to respond.

Well, this is my suggestion. I hope you will engage in positive things and not the things you should let pass.

Bless you.

PROMISES

How often one makes vows, oaths, and promises. How fond of swearing and vowing and promising people are...even to the extent that they require it as a sign of fidelity and trust from others. I say to you that there is danger in making a promise or a vow, for, in some ways, in doing so one energizes that promise or that vow. One takes the energy away from the action and gives it to the promise. So that one, having promised, has discharged the energy and then finds it hard to apply oneself to the fulfillment of the things spoken of.

I have known those who by never promising delivered more than those who promised the Universe. I have known those who by never swearing were more faithful in their trust than those who both swore on Bibles and signed papers of commitment.

If a person means to do a thing, let them keep that uppermost in their mind. Let them not promise it. For then, having promised, they will forget and put something else into their mind. For a promise is a way of dealing with a desire, an idea, or a requirement that says: you must act upon me in some way that is appropriate. Therefore, if you promise to do something about me, or if you swear to uphold me as an ideal, or if you do anything in the nature of a vow of commitment, then you have discharged your duty and need no longer contend with me. Those people who act in such a fashion often find that to be their last good deed in that direction. Whereas those who have not brought themselves to swear, yet have that desire burning within them and that commitment, though unexpressed, will always be felt and therefore it will be acted upon.

So it is , my friends, that to swear is to discharge the energy that would better be kept by keeping silent. To promise is no doubt the thing which sounds good in the doing, but too often proves a burden that prevents one from acting.

I say to you, withhold this desire a little to make these outward commitments. Whatsoever you intend, let it be your intention, and it will move you forward and you will accomplish it. Therefore, the teacher Jesus would have been well advised to say: "Swear not, lest ye be foresworn." And that I hope will be of use to you hereafter.

Peace be with you.

ACKNOWLEDGMENT

I would like to speak to you about the need for acknowledgment. Acknowledgment is, after all, a way in which one gains a sense of effectiveness with others. But it is not the only way. It is one way. And the problem is that one may be very effective, and one may be doing a most excellent job of things and receive no acknowledgment. And if the expectation is to be acknowledged, then the work will not seem to be successful, not to be satisfying and you will feel as though you have not been properly rewarded.

Now it is true that it is important to do something for the love of it, but most people also do things to be loved for doing them. For it is through service that one may acquire a good reputation and the love and the thanks of one's fellow human beings. At least, this is what is hoped for...when, in fact, this presupposes that one's fellow human beings are capable of acknowledgment, have the good sense and the power of observation that enables them to recognize your good works and the good grace to thank you for them...which, unfortunately, most of the time is not the case.

That is because most people are so wrapped up in their own lives and the affairs of their own lives that they spend little time considering what you are up to. And when, in fact, they do have a realization that you have done something worthwhile, they may even in that moment be distracted or dissuaded for one reason or another, from letting you know. Perhaps they are reticent, shy or socially awkward. At other times, they mean to let you know, but forget. And time goes by and the acknowledgment does not come. It is easy to become bitter without those sweet rewards that acknowledgment brings.

If your brothers and sisters in this world are not likely to give you the acknowledgment that is truly due you for what you have done, how shall you know the worth of your actions? How shall you know whether you have been successful in helping them, or that you have indeed done the thing that is good in the eyes of your brothers and sisters? Well, let me tell you some thing...good is not a thing determined by your brothers and sisters, nor is the worthwhileness of your endeavor to be measured by their understanding of it. No, my friends, if there is any feedback, if there is any acknowledgment that you can be certain is always right, it is from your Higher Power. It is from the One who commissions all good works coming through them.

If you would have acknowledgment, seek it of God. If you would have advice or good counsel in the work that you do, seek it of God, not of your fellow men. All too often, they are blind to what you are doing. And even when they have seen it, they are unable to properly evaluate it.

Love is also something that some people confuse with acknowledgment. They hope to get love from others for their good deeds. But if you have love from another, it is not given in exchange for any action. It is forthcoming without having to do anything to earn it, for love is not a thing that is earned. Love is a thing that is received because it is a gift.

And, therefore, you cannot earn your brother's love. Your brother and your sister will give you their love. If they have love, they will give it gladly. And if they have it not, they cannot give it in any instance. They may give approval. They may give affection, but they will not give love unless they have it already. And having it, they will not wait for you to do something to earn it. They will give it straightaway. For that is love's way. So do not be mistaken to think that you can earn love, for love is always a gift.

Now as you become wise, you will realize that the giver is the person of strength, and that he or she who has a gift to give has received this from a Higher Power than themselves. And then, in the act of giving, there will be an acknowledgment from that power which has given the gift that is to be delivered.

And, therefore, as a servant to a Higher Power, you are acknowledged for your service by the One who has given you the work to do. Seek your acknowledgment there, and you will always have it. God will also give gratitude and reward. But of this world, be satisfied with whatever comes to you. And understand that more than this you will need to seek from your own strength and Higher Power.

SELF-INTEREST

You are always acting in behalf of others, when you are acting in your own behalf. If you act in your own best interest, you are acting in the best interest of others...because your own best interest includes the best for others.

Your Shakespeare said it in this fashion: "This above all; to thine own self be true, and it must follow, as the night the day, thou canst not then be false to any man." Which otherwise stated means: By acting in your own best interest, you act in others' best interest. Why? Because if you do anything which is false for yourself or to yourself, then how are you, who have acted wrongly in the first place, able to act correctly in the second place? You are coming from the wrong base. You are coming from error, and it is doubtful that with such wrong perspective you are going to see correctly and act correctly towards anyone else. But many try, of course. They fancy that they will know best for others, even though they have not learned best for themselves.

You know that it is often seen that those who try to live other's lives, for what some would say are altruistic motives, inevitably neglect themselves, and by their neglect, sooner or later, they bring that neglect to the work which they are doing, and sooner or later, self-neglect becomes neglect of duty and neglect of service. And, therefore, whatever they do is flawed and marred by their neglect. Likewise, it is seen that so often in trying always to live for others and to involve one's self in other's lives, that the best energy which is found for one's self is not found from that situation because you are not receiving from others. You are involving yourself in something which does not give to you. It does not return anything to you, and it depletes you.

What you need to realize is that by self-fulfillment, by realizing your own potential, you then are contributing more to the world, because you are bringing out that which you have and enhancing and enlarging it. This is not to be confused with self-serving. This is not to be confused with egoism, but rather it is to value the fact of your existence, to acknowledge that in doing the most with what you have, you are giving the most to the world and maximizing, to use a phrase, your opportunity because you have only to deliver it to the world.

Sometimes you are forced to see others in a light which is less than pleasant, and perhaps you do not want to. And you hide from this. And in hiding from this, you deceive yourself and you also deceive them. You bring a dishonesty to your relationships when you do not wish to see that which is unpleasant. The challenge of life is not merely to acknowledge what is, but also then to resolve it; to deal with it in such a way that it is positively resolved. This is a challenge.

How can one feel a sense of accomplishment if one turns from every unpleasant thing...if one recoils or withdraws? One need not at all. In acting in one's own self-interest, one does not avoid life's conflicts. How is it in your best interest to always run away from things? It is rather in your self-interest to face the challenges of life and to express the truth and the power which is in you. Oh, it is very easy to run away until you find out that you only run into something else. There is no hiding.

There is no ultimate avoiding. One either faces the challenges here or one faces the challenges elsewhere. And what is the difference between facing it here or there? I shall tell you: the difference is merely distance, time and energy... that, of course, which you waste between getting from where you are to the place that is elsewhere. And when you have run a few miles, a few days or years or lifetimes, you come to another spot and face the challenge again. Only this time you are tired because you have been running. This time you are a little less able to face it than you might have been had you stayed where you were. Something indeed to ponder.

Now, I say this, that it is very important to understand what your self-interest is, and that begins with an understanding of your self, which is why I mentioned it in the first place. Because in understanding your self, you understand what your interest is. And that is everything...for without that, what is appropriate...who can know? Only those who know themselves. That is the key to life's action.

Bless you.

HOME

When you have had an enjoyable sojourn, it is just enough of being away to give you a new perspective on old things. Coming home is better, having been away. And perhaps you come to understand the meaning of the word home, more, having been away from it.

Home is a very important place. "Home is where the heart is," your proverb says. Some have said it "is where you hang your hat." But I think you would agree it is where the heart is. There are many beautiful places in this world, certainly many exotic ones, and they are all home to someone. There is hardly a place on the surface of the planet that is not a home to somebody. And when I say that, I say it in the fullest sense, in that it is as much a home as any home could be to anyone.

When you travel, you will come to some places that are very beautiful, and you will say, "Ah, I wish this was my home. I could be so happy here." Stay awhile. You will understand why it is not your home. It will become apparent to you that there is much more to the place than appearances.

On the other hand, sometimes you will go to a place

where it is very poor, very wretched; or it is very cold, or barren, or a desert, and you will say, "How could anyone live here? Why would anyone want to live in such a place unless, of course, they were forced to by poverty or circumstances? Why would anyone choose to want to live here?" Stay awhile, and you will find out why.

For every place has something to give. Every place has an energy, and there is something about it which attracts certain kinds of people. For indeed every place has the ability to provide something. If it is what you need, then it is the place you will feel is your home. If it is not, you will want to move until you find the place that has what you need.

Is a home forever or is it only for awhile? Remember, my friends, that even this planet is only for awhile. So that no matter where you go, where you were born, whatever, that this is but a temporary home. All homes are temporary. They are for a time. and when you understand it that way, it is possible for you to move when the time is right. You do not become fixed or rooted.

Now, there are some who are born in a place and who live in a place their whole life long and who die there and are content. There are some who leave that place and travel around the world but never forget it and always miss it. There are others who are born in such a place, who live there for awhile, but leave it and go someplace else and find a new home. And in finding their new home, they sense that it has much more to offer them than the place in which they were born.

Of all the things that the home gives, surely the most important is the opportunity to share love, to love and to be loved. If you cannot find that in paradise, where the weather is perfect and the food is delightful, what good is that place to you? If you find it in the desert, the desert may seem like a Garden of Eden. Wherever you feel as though people understand and appreciate you, where you are important, where your presence is welcome and where you feel as though others acknowledge you and that your presence is a meaningful contribution, that will be home to you.

For some, it will be in a small place. For others, it will be in a great city. For some, it will be in a place that is wretched; for others, in a place that is beautiful and peaceful. For one, it may be the monastery; for others, it may be the streets, teeming with sickness as they go about their healing work.

You all have a calling. You have a calling not only to service, but you have a calling to a place called home. "Home is where the heart is," where the work is, where life is, where joy is. I know that you will find it.

Peace be with you.

CONTROL

A subject which is near but not dear to your hearts is control. It is, after all, the thing which you are taught from childhood that you must have, and without which your lives will become nothing, and because of which your lives become nothing...which is to say that control leads to a great number of spiritual, mental and physical problems.

You see, my friends, you cannot ever really control anything. It is only an illusion that you can do it in the first place. So right from the very beginning we are talking about *maya*, or *illusion*. Perhaps a better word for control in this instance is delusion, for indeed one is deluded to believe that one can control anything.

Now the fact that many people, if not most people, have from the very beginning always tried to control and even imagined that they could control themselves and others, does not, in fact, mean they ever truly did. It means that they were able to fool themselves into thinking that they had control over the world and the affairs of this planet and over other people's minds and so on and so forth...just because for a time people responded or situations moved in a direction which appeared to them to result from their controlling influence.

Just because people respond or situations move in a direction which appears to be the result of your controlling influence does not mean you have control. It means that for awhile, you have managed to influence the affairs of this world. But control is not by definition of this word a passing, transient influence. It means to truly dominate and to be empowered over forever. It is a thing which will be seen by history and by contemporary experience to be plainly not possible, and yet it is a thing so many people strive for. Like perfection, which is again only an ideal, and at that a very false one...a misconception in the minds of humans about the nature of creation and the Universe that to seek perfection in things is a worthwhile pursuit, so is control also an exercise in futility.

The Greeks had a wonderful story in their mythology about Sisyphus, who would take a rock up the hill, and having got to the top of the hill, the rock would roll down again. This was shown to be an exercise in futility, and perhaps shows us that although humans may seek to arrange the affairs of their lives, those things having once been arranged have a nasty habit of rearranging themselves to suit themselves.

Now a rock is a thing which is more apt to stay in place than human consciousness. And imagine if a rock rolls back down the hill, what it is like to try to manipulate human brains. So Sisyphus had only the frustration of the rock, while others have had the frustration of trying to push others' minds up the hill, only to have them roll down before they got to the top.

There is a need, I suppose, to feel as though one is in the driver's seat. One somehow has some power and is not the victim. Therefore if they can control things, they will control their destinies and they will be free from all manner of negative interference. Somehow, having got control of the whole thing, they will then be free from all unwanted results. But, indeed, those who seem to have risen to the top, who have been empowered by their actions to rule over men and nations, have also had to admit in the final analysis that they could not control their own destiny. They could not control the affairs of the world, just as Napoleon found out he could not control the weather. So it is that even if people think they have control in one area, control is absolutely a false notion.

Well, how does one let go, then, of this false goal...the pursuit of which has caused so many so much pain? What can one seek in its place if one does not have control? What would be satisfying since after all, humans are creatures of questing and questioning? They want always to learn and to develop greater strengths, and that is very well, indeed. And here are the things. Here are the things one might aspire to in place of control.

First of all, one might aspire to going with the flow of the Creator's will. For since in the long run the Creator will have Its way, you might as well go with it rather than against it. And in order to do that, one must surrender a certain amount of autonomy. Because one is forced to admit that there is a power greater than oneself. That such a power exists is rather self-evident if one but looks around. Based upon no religious teaching but simply upon the evidence that one witnesses every day, it is highly suggestive of the existence of some greater mind and greater will. More than that you need not really entertain in terms of the nature of this entity. That is of the very least importance. The fact that there is such an entity, even though you cannot define it (which is another aspect of control), means it exists.

Now, it being there and quite obviously in command and in control of the affairs of the Universe, of the heavens, of the earth and the seasons...it quite obviously must know what is best since it has managed to perpetuate the Universe for all of this time. So one could be a little humble and say, "Well, I trust that that entity knows more than I know." It is just that simple. It is reasonable to suppose that the entity which created me and everyone else knows a little bit more than any of us. That would not be an unreasonable supposition. And here again I say I base this only upon the reasonableness of what is plainly apparent to every eye that is open. I ask no one to accept this upon faith, but upon the evidence that is clearly in front of you.

So if there is a system at work, it is quite obviously consistent, and it is quite obviously able to perpetuate life and order. It has the evidence of an intelligence that is not haphazard or accidental and, therefore, there is something that one can ally oneself with. If you surrender to that Higher Power, do you suppose for one minute that that divine process, which is at work for the purpose of the preservation of life, and has demonstrated itself daily to have the best interest of the planet and all living things as part of its plan, would not want the best for you and direct your life towards its greatest fulfillment? Is it reasonable to suppose that such an entity has decided that you are to make a mess of your life and to fail at everything you do? Is that a reasonable supposition? Is it a reasonable supposition that the entity would want the worst for you? If so, would you have to say "Why?" Why would the Creator create something only to abuse it or misuse it? Would the Creator do such a thing?

Well, we have seen that humans have often abused things and misused things in their great quest for control. They have bent things until they broke. They have warped things.

They have bent themselves. They have abused themselves in the pursuit of power. But the Creator does not do that, for the Creator is not in the pursuit of power, the Creator is in possession of power, and that is the difference: That the Creator is the true authority and the true possessor of power and therefore is in control. And in order to be in control one must have that divine power. One must be as the Creator is...to be able to control. Anything less than that cannot be. It cannot be true.

So how might a simple mortal have any measure of control in his or her life? Well, if one goes with the Higher Power, and the Higher Power controls all things for good and directs them, then you will be directed. You will go with that flow, and your life will start to work out the way you want it to. And I say the way you want it to because you have come to understand that the best way is God's way...the Creator's way.

Now the thing about control that is very inhibiting is that in trying to maintain it, one is always very tight with the reins. They hold on very strongly to every thing and everyone. They grasp, they grip, they clench. They are not open and free. And that posture of tightness and constraint closes the mind, closes the heart, closes the body, closes everything—and not only does it prevent anything from coming out, it most certainly prevents anything from coming in.

There is no thought which may come into a controlling mind for it is a closed mind. There is no love which may come into a controlling heart for it is a closed heart, and no energy for good comes into a closed hand. Certainly there is little that flows out.

So you see that this control becomes that which is the cause of the closing of one's spirit, one's mind, one's emotions. It closes down the one who tries to control it and cuts him or her off from others. And therefore that person becomes less and less and eventually shrivels and shrinks until he or she is too weak to control anything. And the Creator has Its way in the final analysis, which is to say that it is an exercise in futility, like Sisyphus pushing his rock, only it is a very painful one. For those who will not let go must eventually hit a kind of bottom. At this point they lose the thing they tried to have because they are destroyed by their own foolishness.

Again I say it is not that the Creator has willed this for them or desired this for them. It is that the Creator is the sole possessor of true control and power, and ultimately is the only one who can and will direct the affairs of the Universe, and any who try to go against this will come to find out that they are going against the wind. They are going against the force and that force ultimately will have its way.

Therefore, I would suggest, if I may, that to surrender is not to give up one's responsibility in life—quite the contrary. To surrender to one's Higher Power is to take the greater responsibility for one's life by entrusting it to a demonstrably superior intelligence. One has the responsibility to listen, and to follow the directions that that power gives and to do the work which that power requires from those directions. That believe me, my friends, is truly the path of greatest reward and satisfaction. I hope that these observations will be of use to you.

Bless you.

RELATIONSHIPS

Sooner or later you find you end up where you belong. And I tell you, sometimes that is a process of trying out many things first so that you haven't missed anything, or indeed, have missed some things, as the case may be. For if you take the first thing that comes along, you may always wonder if you couldn't have done better elsewhere. So you need to look around, see a lot of things, try a lot of things, meet a lot of people, perhaps be rejected in some places, so that when you finally come to the right situation...whether it is a new job, whether it is a placement of some creative effort, the selection of a new apartment or a place of business, or whatever...you know that what you are getting is good. You know you are getting a good deal, and you feel right about it because you have had something to compare it to. You've had time to see what else is out there.

I wonder sometimes if that isn't one of the things that is the trouble with young marriage: when very young people come together who have not seen the world, tried out anything else...they don't know how to see their marriage. Perhaps they have a very good marriage but they don't know how good it is. And maybe they wonder if there isn't something over the fence...something out there that is better. So, after awhile that curiosity becomes a real compelling interest. After awhile they start to stray away, because they need to satisfy themselves of this question. That is not always the case, but I think that it is many times when they settle for something too soon, before they have enough knowledge to give them that sense of contentment that they know what they're doing. Therefore, a lot of people who have looked around...when they finally settle for something, know what they're getting into.

It is the same way with relationships. After you have had many relationships of various lengths...perhaps you've even had a marriage...you kind of know what you're getting into when you get into a relationship. And although you still have many things to discover, and by no means is a new experience in any way connected to your past, nor should you bring your past into your new relationship, but now you have the ability to discern, to appreciate and to value based on your past experiences, and that is something that cannot be discounted.

Now, many of you are looking for the ideal relationship. You've been around. You are hardly spring chickens. Well, you may think you've missed the boat, even though you haven't, for actually all the relationships that you've had up till now have been necessary so that when that right person comes along, as that right person surely will, you will know very certainly that this is the right person, and you will be able to be very happy and very content and not look beyond that relationship. You'll be content and that relationship will be solid.

So I make that prediction for you, provided of course that you really want to share your life with somebody. But even so, it could still be said about a friendship. It could be said about any person you wish to share your life with. It is also true of your life in terms of service.

Sometimes you don't know for certain that you want to do the work that you've come into this life to do. Although at some point in your life you may have taken it up, you may put it down. You may put it down because you are not certain. You may think that you have to try other things, see other things, or find out if this is right for you. And do not be surprised if some of you come back to things you have tried long ago and of which you said, "Well, I don't find this practical. I don't find any way to do this conveniently, so I'll take up some other work." Many of you have set things on the shelf. Perhaps you will come back to take them off the shelf again and reactivate them.

Sometimes that happens with relationships, believe it or

not when a relationship doesn't go so well for awhile, you go away and then you come back together later in life. You realize both of you have grown, both of you have come to understand things about each other and about life which permits you to come together. It is always very pleasant when that happens. At any rate, don't think that all the intervening experiences are a waste of time. They are very necessary.

If you were to say to me, "Well, I don't want to have a relationship with anybody except my soul mate. I'm going to wait until my soul mate comes," I would say that I think that is a big mistake. I think it is good to have a relationship with whomever it seems possible, provided both people find one another attractive. Although your soul mate is coming, other relationships are very valuable, and they can give you much.

It is the same I would say of someone who says, "Well, I don't want to do anything if I can't do my life's work. I'm going to sit and wait until I can do the thing I've come to do." But I say, "No. Do the thing in front of you. Take the step that is in front of you. Work with what you have, and it will lead you to where you need to be."

It is surprising sometimes how by going in one direction, you find that you go in the direction you had wanted to go in all along, but you had forgotten how to go in that direction.

So by going in the other direction, unrelated, you end up where you belong. It is always that way; you get where you belong.

Then there is the relationship one has with the Higher Power, and there are those who are struggling to find and to maintain a relationship with their Higher Power. This is a very elusive thing, and it can be very unclear in the beginning as to whether this experience is real or something that has been imagined. And you may ask, "How do I connect with this part of myself? How can I receive a relationship with my Higher Power?"

In order to receive the Higher Power within, you must be willing to give up your pain. Sounds strange, doesn't it? You must be willing to give up all of the tools that you use against yourself. You must be willing to give up your vanity. You must be willing to give up your insecurity. You must be willing to give up your feelings of worthlessness or inferiority. You must be willing to give up your anger at not being successful, favored, rich or whatever. You must give up your anger at those who you believe hurt you, or cheated you, or simply failed to understand or love you.

And to do this, to give these up, it is simpler than you might think. It is simply to confess them. It is to cry them aloud and to admit to your ignorance, falseness and vanity and ask that these things be taken from you. It is to admit how foolish you have been, but also to give up guilt. For guilt would take them back again. Guilt would gather them up like fallen apples and tie them on the tree once again to rot. You must leave them and let Higher Power transmute. You must be willing to purify yourself by letting go of all those things you feel you must have. And realizing that everything you need is given to you, so that if you are not a taker, you become a receiver.

For as Jesus said, "Those who have their thanks here have not their thanks there." So, do not look for things but receive them. For the Higher Power is something that comes to those who ask for it, who are willing to admit that they are incomplete without it, that they know that there is something greater than themselves, which until they are part of it, they are not satisfied.

And one must yearn for that.

Bless you.

DEATH

In order to be reborn, you have to die. You have to give up your concepts about how things are and how things came into being and how things are going to be in the future, and let yourself lie fallow for awhile. It is not an easy exercise, and I think sometimes that this is why the Creator has had to help us undertake this very difficult process, whether we like it or not. For death, in its way, makes sure of this, be it a little death, such as that of an idea or a habit, or a big physical transformation happening in the body, mind, or spirit.

Perhaps one might consider using the word change in place of the word death to bring about more clarity, for it is a very natural, if not to say an inevitable act which every thing and every body comes to sooner or later. In fact, death would have to be reinvented were man to take it away through his foolish use of science, not understanding its function in the first place.

So..."To those who are about to die, we salute you." In other words, we celebrate a punctuation in your very long, if not to say infinite, existence...and we accept the decisions of your path. How strange it is that this act of enlightenment should be characterized as going into darkness and returning to the void. But let me tell you, my friends, you are always in the void. You are always part of the void...the All that is and ever was and ever will be. So, what is this fear of returning to something you are always a part of in the first place, life's simultaneity?

The fear of death is often more a feeling of regret. The fear of death is that, having put off what you have come to do on this Earth, it will then be withheld or denied, and the opportunity to do it will pass by forever. But this is not so. Where there is a will there is a way. And your will remains with you as an entity, whether it has a body through which to express or not. You ARE your will, so it is a question of developing enough faith to know that sooner or later what needs to get done will get done.

Yes, sooner or later...if not in this lifetime then in the next, or the next, etc. what you need for your soul's growth will take place. And you will further be able to use these experiences and benefit from the lessons set up by you and for you when the time is right for them to happen.

So do not worry that you will be left out or ignored or forgotten, or any such nonsense, because the Creator is co-creating with you and therefore needs your participation in life's journey in order to learn about Itself.

I hope this will be of some insight and comfort.

Bless you.

THE PATH

There is a tradition in many religions and spiritual initiations that require those who wish to become evolved to give up the world in order to begin a spiritual life. I believe that this is a great mistake, and I want to tell you why I think it is not a good idea, although I know that my belief will go contrary to the teachings of practically every religious practitioner.

When a soul begins to strive for perfection and to desire things of a higher nature, it does so in the midst of the greater world. It is as if one is looking up from the preoccupations of mundane existence and becoming gradually more and more aware of something which is higher. Few, if any, are ready to let go of the context in which they find themselves because they are too insecure to do this. They have attachments which are also supports; things which hold them up, as well as hold them down. And it is very dangerous to sever that connection too quickly.

The new orientation to higher consciousness needs to be gradual, not abrupt. In one who is young and who sees the world as a great opportunity and desires to taste and experience everything and to go everywhere to do everything...this is natural.

So whether it is a young person in one life or just a young soul, there is the need to satisfy this urge. But as the soul progresses, it learns more of life. If it is truly desirous of learning, it will learn. If the soul wants to have more value at less cost, it will start to see that the ratio of satisfaction and price have to be reevaluated. As one gets older and wiser, one sees that it is no sacrifice to set down certain things of this world. In fact, having had one's fill of them, it is easy to say, "Enough!" In fact, it is clear that the life of a spiritual seeker brings him or her to the point where, being older and wiser, the soul craves less and less of this world and more and more of the next world.

So it is not a matter of sacrifice. It is a matter of discernment and maturity. It is a matter of coming to see the true value of things and their proper relationship. When a certain hunger has been satisfied it no longer exists. Another hunger for greater values replaces it...and if the seeker has learned his or her lessons well, when coming to the end of life, one is even prepared to give up the physical body because it no longer holds any great meaning. One is happy to set aside the things of this earth for they no longer hold any charm or grace. Oh, true, there is the sentimental attachment that one has for things that have been loved in one's lifetime or persons who have been loved, but there is also the great sense that they can be re-experienced if necessary in some future incarnation.

The things of this earth which were once very beautiful and very desirable and very necessary for happiness have been replaced with other things of a more transcendent nature, things that are then at a higher plane. So that the jewels of this earth are surrendered for the jewels of the next life: the jewels of higher consciousness. There comes a time when it is natural to exchange one for the other...no regrets. In fact, it is a very happy exchange and one is not deprived of anything—one gains something in that exchange.

There is a very wonderful poem by the English poet, Wordsworth, which addresses many of these points. It is called "Ode On the Intimations of Immortality and the Recollections of Early Childhood". In this poem as an old man he reviews his life experiences and walks once again in his favorite places, but notices they do not have the power over him they once held. They're truly beautiful, he says, but somehow there has been a glory which has passed from them. He is a little sad, only because he hoped that the beauty in them would last forever, for he believed that the beauty belonged to them and came from them. Now that he sees the world differently, he realizes that the beauty was within him. He sees another world opening for him...a new world of higher consciousness. His next spiritual life beyond the physical is that which is more beautiful, more enticing and therefore he is weary of the things of this world.

And so it will be for those who pursue the path of spiritual enlightenment, no matter how materially oriented they are. The danger is that they will give up things too soon and for the wrong reasons. Then it will be experienced as sacrifice and one who has done this may feel, "Ah, I have given up a great deal for this. I have suffered the loss of something for this." Therefore, whatever they obtain will be considered to have been purchased at perhaps too great a price or at such a price that the expectation of what it will provide for them is sometimes unfair and disproportionate.

You have often heard stories of those who have made great sacrifices and then who felt, having done this, that whatever came to them did not somehow compensate them sufficiently. Or perhaps they were looking for something in the act of sacrifice that was not really available to them. It is not the giving up of things that gives the soul any benefit. It is not the act of setting down, it is rather that in choosing new things, one wearies of the old...that one's attraction migrates, shifts or is redirected to things that now have greater value.

When things are given up too soon, there is yet a part within the soul that yearns for them, feels perhaps that they were given up too soon or that their pleasures were not fully explored, understood or appreciated. One wonders, questions, even doubts, whether it was the right thing to have done, and as long as that uncertainty remains within, the soul will want to come back.

What truly enables the soul to leave this life and not come back here? To truly end the cycle of earthly reincarnations is to have fulfilled one's self, not to have sacrificed one's self. Fulfillment requires experience, not the lack of it. Therefore, one must have these things and have one's fill of these things to be truly complete with them.

When the road to spiritual enlightenment and fulfillment begins, it is very wide. It is wide enough to encompass people's life in all its various aspects; their relationships, their material concerns, everything. It is only as it gets close to the point of change into the next life that it starts to become very, very narrow. And the reason that it starts to become very, very narrow is that one by one these preoccupations that were there at the beginning are falling away. The road has narrowed because it has become more focused. It has not been necessary to cover so much ground on either side but to confine one's steps and one's direction to a very focused and clearly discerned point of transition.

I say that so many young people are afraid to make the commitment to spiritual evolution because they are taught that they must give up their worldly existence and life. You know there is a certain religion that requires priests to be celibate, and lately has had a hard time getting recruits. There are other religions that put very stringent requirements upon those who would seek to become enlightened and to follow the true path. And they will not have Universal appeal because they are too forbidding.

Many have asked "Why is it that few people want to become committed to spiritual evolution?" and this is my answer to that question. My answer is my own answer. I do not dream of speaking for the Universe. I do not dream of speaking for God, and I do not speak for religion. I speak for Prahsingh. It is my own observation, and you may discern my wisdom or foolishness as you will. And if you value my opinion in this matter, I would suggest to you that more people would make the attempt if they were given to believe that they were acceptable in the eyes of God *just as they are*. Just as they are...and that it would be worthwhile for them to begin the walk towards higher consciousness without concern as to what they must give up or what they must do, but rather simply to hold it in their mind and in their heart that what they want to do is to become enlightened and to do everything within their power in that direction. And that in doing this it will be given to them to understand what is useful and what is not useful, what is relevant and what is irrelevant in life. They will quickly discern that which is useful, purposeful, that which brings joy and happiness, and that which is only unnecessary and superfluous. Because, as they start to walk on that spiritual path, the priorities of life will become apparent to them. The priorities, of course, that are based on the desire to become enlightened.

It is holding this desire, above all, to become at peace, to become enlightened, to become wise...more than all other things...that will become the program of your path. That will be the blueprint, that will be the direction and sooner or later, as you begin to make your forward progress, all of these other things will become clear. The discernment will occur. Then you will gladly say, "This is no longer useful to me. This is no longer productive. This is not helpful. This relationship is unnecessary..." and so on. It will become clear and, therefore, there is no sacrifice.

There is no sacrifice whatsoever. There is the clear understanding of what is part of enlightenment, what is part of the path and what is not. And that is what narrows the path. The path is seen to become narrower and narrower because what is happening is that the true self is being revealed. The true needs, the true desires and the true nature of happiness itself is being revealed.

So Prahsingh would suggest that you share this with others who may say to you, "Well, I cannot give up everything in life now to become spiritual. I have many other concerns. I have to concern myself with money, my family, this, that... And then I have my own bad habits to contend with..."

Say to them this, "Start the path with your job, your family, your bad habits, money, all these things bring them along, bring them right with you. Let's take it all down the path, and one by one you will sort things out. Don't worry about that now. That is getting in your way, that is preventing you from taking the first step. You're letting the thought of sacrifice stand between you and attainment."

It is very important to try to get people to believe and see that no matter what state of affairs they are in, no matter what their philosophy or belief has been, that the path of enlightenment starts right where you stand at any given moment. And what makes it the path is the desire to have it as the first priority.

You have a teaching in your Bible which says, "Seek ye

first the kingdom of God and the rest shall be added unto you." And I would like to now say it Prahsingh's way, "Seek ye first the kingdom of God and the unnecessary shall be subtracted from you." And when things are removed, you will clearly understand why. Many people will rejoice to find they can start right now to become enlightened without sacrificing anything.

Bless you.

INNER PEACE

I think, my friends, that you lose the state of grace when you lose the ability to relate to simple things.

It is curious to say that you have become very low when you can no longer stoop to touch the grass. When you are too high and mighty to reach down to touch your brothers and sisters...that, my friends, I think is a very low state of consciousness which some call haughtiness. It is an irony, that those who think most highly of their position in life, of their estate and who are proudest, are often lowest in self-esteem. Those who do not count themselves as anything too grand but who are grateful and who reach out as a common member of the human and earthly community, they are exalted in their humility. They are most raised up who are not themselves trying to climb any ladders.

It is strange. It seems as though there is a law of contrary motion at work, that when human nature over-reaches itself and is too ambitious for certain things, it misses the mark. That is a human trait that can be changed. That it is a trait does not mean that one is condemned always to have it. It is simply, how shall we say...an inclination, a predisposition, or perhaps it has to do with karma. In fact it does very much have to do with karma.

But let us not speak now of karma, for that is a great word in which many ideas are too easily lost and swallowed. Let us just speak for a moment of the height of spirituality which is achieved by coming closest to those things which are common, not to feel as though life is lacking...for in having them, one feels full, satisfied and rich.

There are those who must fill every moment with some wonderful experience that is an activity of great and unusual human endeavor. They have not learned to explore the moment with their mind, with their spirit, for what it contains beyond the obvious. They are always trying to make their lives very full of activity. They are going here and they are going there. They're busy and they feel as though their lives are full. But when they sit down for a moment, suddenly their lives become empty. How is it that the fullness goes away? Is it an illusion? Is it that the fullness was only the product of their losing track of their emptiness by so much action? Is it that the fullness never was? What is fullness?

Well, fullness must be that which fills you. And that which fills you cannot be outside of you but must be within you. I submit to you that that which fills you is that which you have after the things of the outer world have ceased. It is that which you have left after your activities are completed. In fact, if there is any fullness, it is that which you keep from the moment, not that which you lose in it.

Strange as it may seem, the moment which is least filled with outside things is most capable of filling one's inside. Because, you see, distractions take from you. They give you nothing. But when one is still, the Universe bestows many gifts, which are otherwise ignored or never seen.

This may sound like a very strange way of observing life, and I do not say that it is easy for everyone to adapt to. It takes a certain amount of willingness to surrender, not to try to control the moment, but to experience it. It takes a willingness to let oneself be raised up and elevated by that which they're experiencing within, rather than that which they are doing outside. But each will come to it in his own time. When the veil of illusion is lifted, the matter I speak of becomes clear.

Those who achieve this inner peace do so because they have surrendered their desires and, therefore, by wanting nothing, have all. For truly it is said that those who reach most, hunger most. Those who strive most, fear most. Those who have the greatest necessity, have the greatest emptiness. Those who have the greatest contentment, experience the greatest fullness, and therefore they are not reaching beyond that which is theirs already to enjoy.

As you become older in spiritual work, you will learn many lessons as you do the work. And as I speak to you now, I reflect upon my own words and I say, "Will it make a difference? Can words be a substitute for life experience? Does what I say remove from you the need to discover the truth of what I speak? What is the value of my saying these things to you if you must come to it in your own way? Are my words wasted?"

No, I think not...for some of you have come to it already, and my words find resonance in you. And, therefore, it is not that I changed anyone's karma, nor is it that I remove from them that which they must do to learn that which they must learn. But to those who have come to this level of understanding I affirm the wisdom which they have gained.

GIFTS

You are given many things by the Creator...life itself! You are given so many opportunities. You are given spiritual gifts, material gifts, gifts of every kind. In fact, the whole planet is a gift to the human race. It is a gift not only to the human race, but to the animal kingdom as well. It is a gift to all who live on it. Moreover, it is a gift that came without any strings attached to it. It is a gift, which means, that as far as the Giver was concerned, no thanks were required, that the Giver did not have an expectation about how this gift would be used. In short, because no strings were attached, you were given something to use and/or to abuse. However, the human race has been oftentimes unaware of the magnitude of the gift, or that it was indeed a gift, which is another matter.

Now as one becomes aware that it is a gift and that one has the power to shape and to change and use that gift, then one feels grateful and privileged for that opportunity. But some people, who are pursuing the spiritual path, make one very great mistake. They do not enjoy their gifts because they feel obligated. They feel a sense of obligation and duty, and they do not experience the joy of living. And no matter how hard they work at what they do, whether it is service or it is creative expression or even worship of God, they can derive no sense of joy. Because their motivation is one of guilt, duty and obligation, they have not the sense of doing it for love, nor for joy.

That your gifts are wonderful can be very over whelming, indeed, when one stops to consider the possibilities of how they might be used. So great is that potential that it may seem overwhelming, and one may feel very sad and unequal to the task. One may indeed feel as though one is not strong enough, not good enough, not worthy of such a gift...that somehow the Creator has made a very bad mistake in giving him or her such a wonderful potential. And, therefore, we resist making any effort to enjoy and to appreciate and utilize this gift, being afraid not to be perfect; not to be what one imagines one must be, rather than what one can be.

It is difficult as one becomes aware of his or her potential. It is so difficult, I know, that many of you must say to yourselves daily, "Will I ever be able to use all of my talents? Will I ever be able to achieve success in the many areas that attract me? And will I be able to get all of the things done in life that seem to be very necessary requirements for just keeping alive in this material world?" Those pressures, those obligations have a way of weighing you down.

This is one reason why many who are on the spiritual

path want to make their lives very simple. We are trying to eliminate as many distractions, as many non essential elements as possible so that we may come down to the enjoyment of some few things to really enjoy them by being able to express them fully, to realize them fully. Because we know that if we are just sampling a little bit of everything, if we are just skimming the surface, we never have the real sense of the depth and power that is contained within something which we have taken our time to explore.

You know it is important, then, to give yourself space and time to enjoy the gifts which you are given. It is important that you not feel obligated to utilize them, but rather that the excitement which comes with appreciation and discernment invites you to take and to delve into the possibilities contained therein.

There is a teaching which has been given that..."Those who remind you of your duty, rob you of your charity." And sometimes you rob yourselves of your own charity. By making yourselves duty bound, you make your lives loveless and joyless. I know it is part of what is called the Puritan work ethic that a thing is of little value if you have not had to work for it. The sense is that a thing is of little value if you have not had to sweat for it and work hard for it. And that is a pity because not everything has to be painful to be valuable.

Some things are just there to be enjoyed without necessarily having to be worked for, although certainly one must work with them. Enjoyment, itself, requires a certain amount of effort, but it is a different kind of effort than one puts forth in duty or through obligation. It is also good for you to see that the Creator, having given things to you this way, is not interested in having you thank Him, but would be pleased if you could enjoy and use what you have. Your gratitude does not make Him the more glorious but makes you able to enjoy what you have received more. Your gratitude is not for God but for you. It is important to remember that. Your appreciation is for you, for without it, you have nothing. It is by gratitude and appreciation that you come to be able to enjoy the gifts which you have and to find their potential for even greater enjoyment.

And lastly, do not give with strings attached, for you will always be sad and disappointed. It is seldom that the world is grateful enough or appreciative enough. Most things which are given take awhile before they can be understood and their value appreciated. So it is with everyone but it comes in time...the understanding of the gift and the value of it. It does not come easily.

But when it comes, then truly there is a wonderful experience which is had, and one wants then to share it with others, so that divine giving is the basis ultimately of all other giving. That God, having given to you and you having understood the gift, then wish to give to others out of the same impulse...which is called love.

Bless you.

LOVE

"Where there is a will, there is a way." And it is so. The will makes the way, and the will comes from the wish. Where is will without a wish? You must not be afraid to dream and to wish. Without the wish there is no will. Without the will there is no way. And who needs a way if there is no wish, anyway?

There is no reason to have a way if one has nowhere to go. So one must want to do something, and wanting is always the first part. But too often people say, "Well, I do not know what I want. Maybe I will find a way to want something. Maybe the way will teach me to wish something." But that is not so. How can I put it?

Love contains desire, the desire to express, for love is no thing, but a motive to make things come into being. Do you understand? Love is not the thing. Love is not the way. Love is the motive that creates the wish which creates the will which creates the way and, therefore, creates ultimately the thing itself.

Some say, then, that love desires nothing. But that is not so. Love desires to express itself in beauty, in healing and helping, in doing things that are wonderful and beautiful. Love desires to make itself known in this world. And how shall love make itself known in this world? By the acts of the Apostles. You, right here, the Apostles of love. That is how it will be known. "You shall know them by the fruits they bear." But so is love known by what it does.

No one learns to love. Love is not an education of that kind. People learn to tolerate one another, but no one learns to love. One is strengthened by love...love just is. If one is filled with love, one loves. One either has or has not love within.

If you have a notion that love, somehow, is an imperfect thing that must grow and become more perfect, then understand that perhaps love is the only perfect thing there is and, therefore, all else must eventually emulate its perfection. However, you will quickly understand that much that passes for love isn't. What many feel is love in them, is mere affection or yearning or desire. So how can you distinguish between these things?

Love is the want of nothing and the having of all. Love lacks nothing and provides everything. Therefore, love is full and complete. It seeks nothing. It wants nothing. It has all. Love merely is, and it is a power that motivates all other actions. It releases one from need. Therefore, it is never small. It is always great. It does not grow, but all things grow from it, for it is like manna that feeds. It is not the food that grows, but the one who eats it. Those who are fed by this food grow from it, but it does not grow. It is the eternal source of power.

It is very easy to confuse many other feelings with love. Some confuse it with mere enthusiasm, others with passion, some with adoration, others with respect, some with need, others with affection. Love does not need and certainly does not need to tolerate. For toleration, as condescension, is something that abides, but not gladly. Love is glad, even in the face of iniquity. It neither tolerates nor abides but acts appropriately. There is nothing about love which endures iniquity, and everything about it which acts to right it and make all things in its image. Love is not abstract. Love is very real. That is to say, love is an energy that motivates and a consciousness. It is a power.

So if you are without inspiration, or if you find you have not a good idea, if you have not enough will and certainly no way, then go back to love. Yes, love is that from which all things can spring. For what is love? Ah, love is the Spirit itself. Love is the essence of life. Love is to be, as death is not to be. Simply, to be. How many of you know how to be? In being is love. Love is being. If you do not know how to love, then try to be, and you will love. Because you cannot be without loving. You cannot love without being. They are alter egos...synonymous. To be is to love. To love is to be.

What does it mean, to be? Ah, the great question is as mysterious as "What does it mean to love?" It is a mystery because it cannot be intellectualized. It can only be experienced. What it means cannot be part of a thought process. It can be part of an experiential reality. Therefore, being means experiencing and allowing experience of one's whole being, not just one set of realities, but the whole reality...the emotional, the spiritual, the intellectual and the physical altogether...allowing these things to provide for one that which is called knowledge.

Knowledge, true knowledge, is that which is understood by all of this, all of this loving and being comes down to an understanding. It comes down to ultimately some form of intelligence: innate, inherent, which is the product of the experience, and the experience has stimulated this awareness. So loving can also be called allowing one's self to experience, and it is, above other things, not judging.

Knowledge is there, and questions are answered before they are asked. Because, let me tell you, the world provides all the answers without the questions. The questions are not necessary. The answers are there. Because if the answers were not there, the questions would not help you. So why bother with questioning? Listen more and get more out of life. You take too much time to question. Do more listening because it is there without questioning.

This is what I think of being. Being is not questioning. Being is being aware. Or, as someone once said,
  "Let the butterflies light on you rather than to chase them."

Well, I hope I have made my point. I hope I have helped you along your road to consciousness, and I am happy to be here with you, my old friends.

Blessings, blessings, blessings, many blessings, abundant blessings, exceedingly abundant blessings.

I am Prahsingh.

To order this book

Visit our website:
www.theroadtoconsciousness.com

or Call: 845-379-1080

or Write to:
Manitou Publishing
P.O. Box 422
Garrison, NY 10524